We Pass Each Other on the Road:

Fantastic and Real Encounters

We Pass Each Other on the Road:

Fantastic and Real Encounters

Poems by

Hanoch Guy Kaner

Cover design by Shay Culligan

ISBN: 978-1-63980-050-6

Kelsay Books
502 South 1040 East, A-119
American Fork, Utah 84003
Kelsaybooks.com

*dedicated to all the people I met along the road
and the characters I invented*

Contents

Cocoon

Snowstorm in the valley,
Vermont childhood comforts—
sledding to school
our Volkswagen Beetle
encased in ice
at the bottom of the hill
coming home to
the wood stove heat,
wiping the window,
catches a glimpse
of eleven-year-old Annie
in a yellow coat.

Noisy birds and cars—
winter magic gone.
Pure white taken over
by blue and green.
Trudging to school through mud,
in a snowstorm, I cocoon
in a dream of pleasure.

Not documented

in 18th century deed ledgers,
and glad it's not.

It knows it is over a hundred twenty years old.
Has no recollection of the 19th century.

Weary, bored, anxious—and fearful
it will slide into the creek,
carried away to the Delaware.

Dislikes the name "house."
Fancies to be called Guy Mansion
but rejects it in favor of
a balloon, a cloud,
at least a colorful ball
on the roof.

Snow
makes it helpless:
it can't repair a broken branch
or help up an elder who fell,
can't bury a tiny pigeon.
Has no hands to pat dogs.

Hummingbird
unnerves the house.
Its fast wings make it

faint and graceless.
It prefers the hawk
quietly diving for a mouse.
Crows crowding on a pine,
creating a racket.

Sarah moves to Heaven's Cradle

Two large fake bougainvillea plants
At the entrance lead to a large common room.
Two bay windows look on the garden,
Chinese vases on the round tables.

Grey double doors to the
Guests' rooms.

I am eighty years old. Ilya's my friend.
My room by the broom closet.
Men's room on the other side.

My daughters skimped and saved.
Put me in Heaven's Cradle.
I've seen a doctor only once.
He was bored.
Prescribed a laxative.

I press the button:
Nothing.

The nurse watches a get-rich game show.
Mort screams in the other room
Through a toy phone for pepperoni pizza—now!
Sean cries—no vanilla ice cream.
The floor attendants drag
A crumpled shroud.

I shiver in a thin gown,
Tear the screen and fall
Onto a wet lawn.

Innkeeper Sue

One morning she found herself
in the kitchen cooking
a soft-boiled egg
for a gentleman from Britain.
Then running out of coffee
in mid-breakfast.
Hard to remember how she got here.
A young Italian couple stumping
up the stairs after midnight.
Indian newlywed tracking
Bryce Canyon red mud.
And an aspiring poet
spreading gravel from
Zion Virgin river.
She's never left the inn
but bursting with suggestions
for Utah travel.

63rd Birthday

A coreless country collapses
into tar quicksand.
Lost between
King Herod red marble columns
in Caesarea,
the Western wall,
and the Dead Sea.

King Solomon's empire zeal
burns in occupied territories settlers
who, waving Torahs, uproot
ancient olive trees.

At 63, the State celebrates
its victories.
Wars
defeating memories
of pogroms, martyrs
and Masada
by reversing victimhood.

Tel Aviv's bars filled
With revelers and hookers.
Palestinian refugees storm through cacti fields
in the Golan heights on the Syrian border.
Beaches overflowing
with sun worshippers.

Hidden by sandstorms,
Bedouins crash through Rafa'
crossing at the Egyptian border.

In hundreds of small boats,
they land at Jaffa's port.
Thousands of camels and sheep
break through the Jordanian border,
madly driven by a harsh east wind.

Mel Brooks and associates

It is all a big mistake:
They call it myth but it's a stupid error.
Lord Frankenstein was never a Lord.
Dracula was never a Count.
All lost in the transmission or translation
by a toothless old Romanian horse thief.
His name was Igor. Or was it Max?
Frankheim or whatever was his name
lived in rural Pennsylvania not Transylvania.
His cousin Drake was ridiculed around these parts
by the name of Drak-Ulaf
Because he was never so bold enough
as to speak to a maiden.
His cousin was a blood sucker.
But his name was never known.
Anyway, Ulaf and his brother Frank
were big on eating fungus off the rocks
till the green came out of their nose.
Greennose the shepherds called the two.
Then they would gorge on red mushrooms
Which left their mouths dripping red
Well, you can guess the rest.
Mel Brooks got hold of the story
and bought the movie rights.
The Ulaf Frankheim clan wanted to sue him.
But by the time it got to court all were dead.

Then Romania broke off the Soviet block
and badly needed cash.
So they promoted castles and caves in Transylvania
as the places Frankenstein and Dracula roam.

And they recruited virgins to scream hysterically,
smeared with makeup, and ugly actors to chase them.
Meanwhile, Yvonne DeCarlo invented *The Munsters*
with Herman who was too tall to be employed.
It's all a big mistake.
That too is to become a myth.

Hell

for R. Z. Back

The stuffy tent wreaks of urine and sour sweat.
Ya Ahmed Mahmud, ibn al-Sharmuta, son of a whore.
Sammy's shiny boot in the blindfolded officer's stomach.
How many soldier guns? How many sluts?

Ten tanks in the valley.
A hundred soldiers in the village.
Just two guns on the hill. Sluts?
Sammy kicks him in the gut.
Lie, tell the truth,
it's all the same to me.
The tall prisoner leaks
blackness down to pale tied feet.

Morris picks his nose, wipes it on the contorted face.
Moss digs between his gold teeth with a toothpick.
You ibn al-Kalb, dog's shit.
The prisoner's nose bleeds on his torn hands,
I am bored, Sammy says, spitting.
Shurbat maya—water! whispers the prisoner.

Sammy bursts out laughing
Moss, kick the nothing in the balls
It's an order.

The prisoner flies out of the tent,
lands face down.

Sammy winks to Moss:
I don't feel like filing a report.
Let's empty a round in its back.
Shot trying to escape like the other four dumb animals.
That's what we tell the captain, hell with him.
Throw it into the wadi.
The crows deserve another treat.

He burps.
This damn sand is everywhere.
Let's go to lunch.

Saul and Glioma

Ten thousand astrocytoma troops
crash down, ten thousand glioma tumors
parachute into his cortex. Tens of thousands
of tumor-troops swarming throughout his brain.

Slowly Saul adjusts his hearing aid.
His group mates' stories
sound softly as a lullaby.
He rocks from side to side as
Thomas talks about travels in Tibet
and James starts singing a nursery rhyme:
"The Duke of York marched his troops
ten thousand strong up and down the hill
with Duke Barak, up and down,
up and down Mount Tabor."

Up and down Saul moves his head,
Up and down glioma tumors slide and climb.
Up and down, Saul listening to
Judd's story about the lovers
suspended in a bubble.

Doc Rosen shoots at him quick:
"Glioma, oligodendroglioma, astrocytoma, glioblastoma."
"Doc, stop! Please! These are more fitting names
for Egyptian princesses who were desired and cursed

by the lustful God Ra, blessed by Isis
and turned into necklaces of stars
in the far reaches of the Milky Way."

Saul rolls down the mountain together with his group mates.
He takes out his hearing aid and dances on his knees,
chanting: "Ten thousand strong in my skull,
up and down the hill, up and down Mount Tabor."

Saul, cuddling his head, remembers:
"My love, hug me inside the bubble."

Seven Pillars

Seven pillars of cancer
established their thrones.
Seven glioma pillars on mounds
of thick gray mass.
Seven pillars of cancer's god
look over fissures full
of chewed-up spit-out gray matter.

Seven gods command the neurons
and circuits: bow and surrender.
Blinking blinding lights hit the skull
from all directions, setting the cerebrospinal fluid
on fire, scorching the cerebral cortex.

The right hemisphere collapses over the corpus callosum,
uprooting axons, piling them up on the steps of the frontal lobe.
Extinguishing sounds and deafening eyes.

Seven pillars collapse, spontaneous fires ignite.
Destruction and devastation consume my cities, roads and gardens.

My love sinks into the rubble,
hugs me in a blind cavern.

Never trust

a man dressed in black,
Victoria said to me herself,
her retainer twinkling
at Harold across the table
in the Biblical Hebrew class.
The stories of lusty David
are leaving her short of breath.
She rebuttons her blouse
to restrain her breasts,
It's a summer course.
Harold removes his black jacket,
looks at her through his thick glasses
and a thin moustache.
Victoria smooths her blouse.
Shall we review for the test together?
asks Harold. She shoots back:
I never trust a man wearing black,
even if he is a lay minister.

Evening

Two roommates,
eyes half open.
Big shaved heads.
Very light bodies
easily lifted
by a nurse turning the bed.
Each one emits monosyllabic
sounds in turn.

Evening
descends on the dunes.

Joe's widow

came running from her house across the creek.
"Did you see my Joe, my brave Joe?
Who battled Parkinson disease
till a flu-like virus attacked him, poisoned his liver.
Did you see him?
I have many questions for him.
I am sure he did not lose touch."

While Peggy, the widow from across
the street, dragging her gray white
puppy, went to and fro, skidding within
shadows to the creek, pleading,
tugging at angels' robes.

"Did you see my Joe?
he was here
just a moment ago.
I have to ask his advice.
He should help me decide.
He knows."

A poet

rushes into the world
to displace a dead brother.
a bullet lodged in his crib.
a mouthful of toothless *whys.*

born with Isaac's knife in the kishkes.
waiting for miracles in gas chambers,
settles for crumbs.

hugs the walls blinded by the sun,
crawls in the dirt, caught in barbed wire.
smashes darkened windows.

warm nights find him in an olive tree
watching hurrying scorpions,
joining the jackals' mournful howl.

sleeps in a mulberry bed tickled by silkworms.
gorges himself with sticky purple berries,
he is in the council of owls.
a red fox befriends him.

drinking the first fall rain,
he is surrounded by young snails,
serenaded by tiny wagtails.

dumped by an army driver in the desert.
crows viciously attack sparkling shards.
Egyptian vultures circle above.

A poet too

is startled by black birds on the bridge
taking off as a tank roars.

still carries his dog Sam that was put to sleep in his arms.
shoes caked with red clay from his parents' cemetery.
keeps empty frames for his Romanian grandparents.

dislodges a feeble god off his back,
throws him a penny.
chases out a quire of noisy angels
for a naked muse.

commas, periods leave him indifferent.
semicolons out of the question.
willing to compromise on capitals.
appalled by possessives.

on his last journey
his knapsack full of blue desert,
the Rio Negro, a snowy Teton peak
and orchard blossoms.

Bilbo Picaro,
sporting a hawk's red feather in his hair,
ready for new adventures.

It becomes

It becomes slowly but surely a
habit of dodging when a swift
blow approaches like a U.F.O.
This is what it is, son.
It is not like the old masters-apprentices
in Venice and Florence or Japan
copying strokes for days and nights.

It's more like fishing in a dead
North Dakota lake.
It is the painful delight of drinking
broken spinal cord juice.

ABCDEF. K.

A
My other smashes the jar
Goes back to womb
Strangles mother with the cord

B
Beyond the mirror
my unborn twin freed
from curses of down syndrome,
stunted growth and horrid face.

C
My other kid retrieves
my painted wooden horse
takes off above the heavy blue
rides a feathercloud

D
My double—careless, clumsy
burns soup and stove
forgoes Monday's yoga
Thursday's poetry
Lies in the grass
gobbling worms

E
My other elders
release me from ALS dementia,
indignities of begging
obnoxious male nurse
to be taken to the bathroom.

F
My others don clown suits,
kick me with oversize sneakers.
Gag me.
Throw me up.
I crash
right into the fire
roasting
with an apple in my mouth.

K
A man
with short legs shuffles
every morning past your window.
Franz shoots you a hateful look.
You slam him against the stonewall,
pity him, throw strudel crumbs,
torment him with your stories.
He still wants to kill
your Yiddish theatre lover

married to a thug.
He is Moishe the beggar.
No relation to Moses.
You're both forced into

an out-of-control wagon racing
down to the Penal Colony.
I will have to change,
I guess.

Rushing past the guards
up the castle staircase—
I guess you have to change.

Joel walks

in the park
every day at 5.45 am.
Waves his arms upward,
kicking his feet.
ignores dogs, people,
greets Eli warmly:
Here you are, old timer?

He walks against
his bandaged feet, lost thumb, his cane.
Bends to pick up wrappers, cups, bottles.
Throws them into separate bags,
Sons of bitches pigs.
Joel walks violently in the park
at odds with the litter,
his bandaged feet, lost thumb,
lost love at Paris airport.
Still hears the whisper:
Come with me to Israel.

Waving his arms upward,
at odds with his cane,

Dizzy, slips on a patch of ice
Goddamn me
These sons of bitches pigs

Empties the wrappers, glass and plastic bottles
into the right cans.
Waits for his ride to
the brain radiation session.

What do Susan and Bob do?

What do Bob and Susan do?
All day and night in their big house.
Eight bedrooms and four and a half baths,
two decks, one second floor porch
and an eighteen-by-ten swimming pool.
No kids nor pets except a raccoon family in the old oak
and an arthritic relative who comes to their Thanksgiving dinner
and walks in the pool during the summer.

What do Susan and Bob do?
In the dark second and third floors
and the dim lighted first floor where
I can see them both bending
over a huge table at the bay window.
They paint their house off-white every two years,
hire a gardener in the fall and spring,
put on the air conditioners from April to October
and heating from November to March.

Every two years they buy identical cars,
always a Honda SUV.
April to October they go on walks
on Mondays and Thursdays evenings.
Every year just a touch of more gray in their hair.
He is more bent and she is still talking softly.

We exchange questions:
How is your family,
How was the summer fall winter spring?
How is school?
Good seeing you.
You too.

What do they do the rest of the time?
In their eight bedrooms,
the dark second and third floors,
their four-and-a-half baths,
the swimming pool,
the sundecks,
the porch, new cars.
the dim lighted front room.

And what would they do?
When the snow buries the sundecks,
fills the second-floor porch.

When the scorching heat shuts off the air-conditioning,
scorches the grass, wilts and kills the water lilies.
Dead black-eyed Susans at their front door
and in the pool. And
the gardener never comes.

Raus

He is dragging furniture
in his former workshop.
Groggy, I open the door.
A truck takes off.
Oil stains, metal shavings
all over the floor.
Black truck tracks.
Your truck is gone for thirty year.
Burly Hans is dressed in a grease-stained coverall,
heavy flannel shirt, worn out work shoes,
metal framed glasses.
Red faced he grumbles
My workshop is full of junk
I resent you moving the kitchen cupboard
From the middle to the south wall
I dislike the green room
Can't stand the apricot paint in the bedroom
He shoves a fist in my face. He grunts.
You let the front lawn grow into a jungle
My gardener Mike took good care of it

—I like the jungle.
It is none of your business.
Go where you belong.

Hans is curled in the crawl space.
He plays with my wife's old glasses,
my expensive sunglasses.
Jingles silver dollars I was looking for.
Sweeps the basement.

When are they bringing the coal?
—Coal? For seventy years, they don't use coal.

He hisses under his breath,
Raus! Out of my house!

My wife jabs me in the ribs—
You are talking to Hans again!

Ribbons and bows

Adair
out of the incubator
a bow on your tiny diaper
new crib
shiny wrapping
ribbons all over your room
shiny wrappings
holding on to your crib bars
struggling for breath
ribbons in your blonde hair
boys pulling on them

clutching gray fists
hospital tubes replace ribbons

oak casket
red bows on top

the wolves were circling

they didn't howl or pounce
snow held its breath
and cleared a path
five-year-old Seglana
left grandmother on the floor
runs out the door
crossed the forest in fright
and frozen walked three miles
to her neighbor Arkady
on a snow mobile the country doctor rushes
grandma cold on the cold floor
grandpa howls from the grave
grandma's house covered by
heavy cruel snow in Siberia
Seglana rushed to the hospital with the flu
the wolves were circling

Heil to Heavy Metals

O let us treasure heavy metals, our sacred substance!
Babies' blood saturated with mercury—
morning and night
they drink metal skies,
they suckle corroded pipes,
they lick the lead earth as ice cream.

Be proud of your waterways enriched with antifreeze.
So proclaims Dr. Jeremiah Max Fraudham
of the FDA, FTC, AMA and Astra.
Everything is fine, he assures us,
levels are perfectly safe.
Animal studies in which mortality
was a mere five percent prove it.
No significant harm has been done.
The industry regulates itself remarkably.
The President dances at the White House
with Jeremiah's red head mistress,
pinching her cheek—oh, bubbele!

Meanwhile Sir Jeremiah is promoting praises
of unpredictable changeable qualities of heavy metals
creating low clouds over Iraq, Iran, California and Sweden.
Reverend Pat Robertson exhorts his faithful:
I proudly support heavy metals.
It is our duty as Americans to consume
heavy metal-enriched water, food and air,
which make us the strongest nation in the world.
The arrival of the metallic age is clear.
It is written in the Book of Revelation:
Metals will prevail.
Metalle machen dich frei

Jeremiah Max meanwhile is promoted in the Church
of Heavy Heavenly Metals and now leads the liturgy
for angelic acid rain, torn ozone, flying chemical debris,
and glowing, fume-belching blue babies orbiting the earth.
He exalts the new UBERMENTSCH,
hyper-enriched with copper and selenium cadmium.

In a mad ecstasy of concentrated bioaccumulation,
Jeremiah Max, foaming at the mouth, wetting his pants,
throws himself into a toxic dump in Nevada,
screaming: *Ich bin der grosste Schaffer!*

Ubersurgeon

Steady knife cuts,
slices splices.
Nimble fingers
saws thin lines.
Incision unseen.

He amputates a leg or a hand.
Articles, buts and pasts
land in the toxic waste bin
with commas and conjunctions.
Scattered lone limbs stand proud.

Triple-spaced grace.
Stitches dissolve.
The poem is whole.

California and Clay

Like a thief I snuck
into Bill's studio.

For a long while I spied on him
making a huge white clay jar.
In the dead of a February night.

I grabbed onto ear-shaped handles
and jumped in. He watered the jar
and quenched my thirst.

Come April he'd gone.
On vacation, and spring brought in
busy birds chirping and a pair of robins
nesting under the eaves.

I fell asleep and woke up
to summer's end and heavy rains.
Fall decorated the windows
with colorful leaves.

Months went by.
Bill redonned his apron,
hollered to his neighbor Bob.

They loaded the jar into the truck.
I lost my balance and fell.
Stared into Bill's eyes.

Here, my little friend:
a sandwich for the road
to California—*zay gezunt*.
Bon voyage.

Reverse laughter

double bypass at forty-five diabetes at fifty
back surgery in a month I still have my vegetable garden—
I am too young to be old

Talking blues: Great Uncle Philip

A broken bottle
Stick menacing
Alley cats
Narrow red eyes
Beard stuck in toothless mouth
Makes babies shriek
Goes out in torn sandals
His pajama pants dragging
In December
Sneaks into the morgue
Uncovers sheets
Delighted
To see
Old friends
Gets mugged
And shot at 3 am
At the Q station
Joins
His friends
At the morgue

Queen Sheba's Harvest

Pale virgins at the harem bathe me
in pomegranate essence and myrrh, then
Tiberias mud and Kidron spring foam after.
They marvel and giggle at my deep dark skin.
Frightened by my panther eyes.

Autumn lights and shadows alternate
on the Temple's brown marble walls.
Along the paths handsome priests
with red beards in blue striped white
rush up the hill with calves.
Sweaty Arabian stallions gallop. Even
the chilly Jerusalem night cannot cool my lust.

Tall Hittite mercenaries gather round
my wrinkled eunuchs fascinated by their
desert tales of fighting dragons, camel races
and treasures in caves. They covet my women guards
and their precious stones studded daggers.

Veils whirling to tambourines
in the midst of quail and lamb feast
and a duel of riddles and parables.

Finally, I am summoned before the harvest pilgrimage.
First Queen Abigail offers me to the King.
I am moon radiant.
My black hair snakes.
Rubies and emeralds at my feet.

At the feet of the lion
by the throne—
I trip and fall.

Talking Blues: Promise

At 90,
I catch a lucid moment—
to tell you, Mary:
You're 70.
Soon
mini-strokes will
rob you of decades.

Every five minutes
you pester
the cleaning lady.
Give me the test results.
Give them to me
now!

On Wednesday,
you wander the village
on your walker
sucking a lollipop.

A crate full of dentures
gawks at you:
Postage due.

Willie to Willy L.

Willie
The sun beats on, cuts my face
Winnie is buried up to his chest
—with his ridiculous straw hat
Chatty and cheery

Does not allow me to crawl
into my hole unless I look at her
My mouth full of the chalky rock
her auburn hair lit

Besieged by hungry mouths—
your failing arteries complain
The grass on our street is burned by cars
Why do you keep buttoning my shirt to my neck?
I'm suffocating

I broke into Timmy's piggy bank
Pawned Andrea's nice boots and coat
I spent a night in the attic tearing my teddy bear
You don't understand, not ever having kids

We'll make a killing in the rich timberland
I bought for pennies in Alaska
The bosses in the company
love me and I will get a bonus
Bills and evictions notices are piling on the table

And the fridge is empty
My son is Lucky
My daughter Happy
If I only had the guts to kill myself

Envoi

Oh Willy,
if you'd just spend a short day
in my hole and look buried—
you'd count your blessings

Our flesh melts in the sun
We fall like old dogs
and the searing buzzer
in the withdrawing light
is our savior

Samson

A long time ago, in a village
far away in the mountains,
Samson, the village idiot turned thirteen.
Rabbi Lamb went attired in fox skin hat
and with his trusted hunchback aide
to talk to Reb Chai, the lucky father.
After a glass of schnapps,
The good rabbi told the father
to prepare the boy at least to read the Sh'ma'.
At least the Shema' our law requires,
and may be the Barekhu.
The boy's mother, Feiga, small and skinny,
let out an alarming wail,
joined by grandma Miriam and
the spinster daughter, Zelda,
they chased the rabbi and his aid
who ran from the house without a word.
"This rabbi's belly is full of books
and oral law but empty of compassion.
His common sense is
like our poor son's."
"What the rabbi said has to be done,"
Said Reb Chaim.
"At least the Shema'."

On the appointed day, the boy was brought to Shul,
hugging his pillow and double wrapped in diapers.

Thick silence wrapped the congregation.
By the holy ark the father sat.
By him his bulky son sucking his thumb.
The scroll of Torah open on the lectern,
waiting for the blessings.

while the boy's sweat reddened his pimples.
When the father and the rabbi mouthed a *sh, sh,*
the boy was busy catching flies.

The father began blessing the Torah,
pushing his son whose lips curled attempting
sound. But what came out was
pa-pa-pa, then he started crying,
ran to his grandmother in the women's section
and plopped his heavy bulk in her frail lap,
almost toppling her over.

His mother cried and took him
behind the curtain to clean him up.
The bar mitzvah boy had joined
the minyan, at last.

rushing past the guards,
  up the castle staircase

1.
I am suffocating in the safes
in Zurich and Tel Aviv.
Again my tyrant father tortures me.

2.
I cried and pleaded with Max:
burn every piece of paper with my writing.
He betrayed me.

3.
Now these two spinsters have their hands
at my throat threatening to publish everything.
You owe it to the world of culture.

4.
I owe nothing to lowly ignorant bureaucrats
filling useless dusty ledgers
with claims to be married to K.

5.
Let the safes ignite.
Burn down the banks.
Like Joseph K.—
I wait.

offshore

Rosalind sank into bed, exhausted.
The hum of the generator downstairs
and the Polish nurse singing
a lullaby to Charles.
His oxygen tank whistles.

She drifts offshore,
dives through clear water,
bends under a mossy rock.
Wakes up with a start.
Salt sparkles in her window.
Glasses clatter noisily to the floor.
The generator stops,
oxygen line silent.
The nurse is gone.
On her palm,
a tiny pearl.

scents

You are scents
of clay birth soil,
childhood yard eucalyptus leaf
imprinted on your chest.
Mounts climbed
in your leg muscles
join memory streams
of Rachel's aloe shampoo.
Perfume bursts, lilies and jasmine,
a carpet of orange blossom
hugs your feet.

Decades pass.
Dusty roads dull senses.
Scents fade.
Face smoky greasy
in tank wars
on the northern mountain
and the southern desert.
Each flag raised,
skin shriveled.

At last a gentle light with
a sudden purple wind
embraces him,
fragrant and fresh.
As in the moment of birth.

Silver cord, golden bowl

Mourners go about the streets…
before the silver cord is loosed,
and the golden bowl is shattered.
                    —Ecclesiastes: 12:5–6

41 boxes.
I counted them a week ago,
when after 5 years I moved back in
with Trudy.

That Monday morning, disoriented,
I wake at 4.00 am.
It is as if I went to India again,
driving to the airport through columns of snow.
Only this time my Uncle Jack
drives us to the hospital.
Trudy's surgery is at 6.00 am.
They will open her and take out
uterus, cervix and tubes.
"100% of her cancer will be out,"
said Doc Reznitz confidently:
"Of course, pathology
has the last word."

I stare at a beardless face in the mirror.
Matt is teaching my advanced seminar.
Each night I sleep on a cot in her room
between tubes and monitors.
We are driven home
again through columns of snow.
I sleep in the den surrounded by 41 boxes.
At 3 am I get up to look.
She is breathing.
She will never be Trudy.

Trudy's hair is back.
Her eyebrows came back first,
Then her scalp, covered
with a two-day stubble.
By the end of the week,
the soft plume of a baby.
In another week she had
A crew cut. Wow.
Her hair is back.
She we went to the park without her wig,
She may go to work without it.
It is a miracle.
It's back.

We thought.
We drove.
We went on walks.
We went out.
The cancer went in.
Mornings after chemotherapy:
lawyers, living wills, advance directives,
power of attorney,
hospice talks.
Four and a half months—
maybe.

After the party
for all our supportive friends,
Trudy rests on the easy chair.
Her eyes closed,
dozing. Party leftovers
neatly packed in the fridge.
Enough for three weeks.

Trudy hugs a pillow. describes energetically
her trip to Lake Superior: the blooming blue flowers
in the rocks' tranquility, singing trees surrounding
the lake, the serenity of the inn.
She falls asleep hugging a pillow over
her cancer soup swollen belly.

Most of the time Trudy is cheerful.
She says: It's been an incredible year.
Thirty people held a Rosh Hashanah service at our house.
On Sunday, the choir came, twenty strong,
and gave an hour-long concert.

Most of the time she is cheerful.
She managed to write her
monthly article for the college journal.
She rehearsed her funeral with rabbi Rochelle.
I did not talk with her about the arrangements.
I need to do that.
Live your life fully, she tells me.
Do not go to brunch with an old friend.
Do not schedule anything on Friday.
You need to swim.
I am thinking about Thanksgiving,
confusing it with the day she would be gone.
Trudy scolds me, wagging her finger at me:
These are two separate dates!

She has a room full of gifts:
Future birthday and anniversary gifts.
She sent a card for her friend Joan
That arrived a week after her death.

She bought eight gifts
for Hannukah for our daughter.
She put a note on a blanket
for the birthday of our grandson.
My daughter, who does not even
have a boyfriend, looked at me.

On the thirtieth day, Trudy's friend Ann
gave me a letter that Trudy wrote
two weeks before her death.
I will be given another letter
On February 10th,
three months after her death.

One afternoon,
she opened her eyes,
looked at me mischievously,
went on to list all my women friends,
describing each one's qualities to a tee.
She analyzed whether we are compatible,
remarking she is an objective matchmaker.
I could not say a word.

I keep a vigil:
Hovering over her bed,
trying to see beyond her glasses,
holding her hand, falling asleep by
the huge hospital bed filling the "leaving room"—
that's what she called it.
On Monday morning, I leave my post,
go upstairs to brush my teeth,
splash water on my face,
leave my glasses upstairs.

I come back—
she is gone.

I called with an unsteady calm voice
to my daughter: Hannah, Hannah.
She pushed hard against my chest.
Trudy had prepared a check list.
We followed it.

All of a sudden out of my foggy tiredness
the room steadied itself, the light clear
and the branches in the east window shined.
The telephone rang and rang
together with the doorbell.
The room was full of friends
The room was empty.
She rose quietly and stood
by the east window looking
at the cypress branches.

She died,
again and again.
First, on the day of the diagnosis.
Second, from fear of the surgery.
Then with each chemotherapy.
On a balmy September day
the relapse arrived—
another death.

She came alive at the party for our friends.
Then died again when we put
the hospital bed in the leaving room.

I shared all her deaths.
Except the one on November 10th.

My daughter Hannah and I
walked her to the corner.
We stopped, but she kept on going.

We scattered her ashes,
as she requested,
over the west park.

In twelve places we scattered them
between the bench and the covered bridge.
Carefully I removed snow and leaves,
covered the ashes with snow and leaves,
so involved with the mechanics,
I did not know what I felt.

I recited a hurried
free translation of the Kaddish.
A rain storm roared through.
As I walked away
I looked back:
Trudy was rising
and pervading.

My heavy steps turned
into light steps,
the empty box in my hand,
and I a vaguely remember
a Russian princess wandering
over the hills and into the woods
with a box that held a secret name.

a hundred words

Name a bird an ant or food,
tree or dry flower—
white coat tells me,
blinds me
with a light in my eye,
hits my knee with a rubber hammer.
I look at my wife
You know a hundred words, she says.
Fuzzy pictures rush through.
The piano plays.
Kafka drops by.
I know his bald red head.
His hand shakes.
His lips move German syllables.
Pupils racing around puzzled eyes.
Shirt sweat stain.
I don't know if the tea cup
is his or mine.
I drink it quickly.
So he won't grab it.

A mountain of mail
on the kitchen table.
The phone rings.
Somebody keeps banging
on the door.

I am furious at my wife
for not teaching me
more words.

Books by Hanoch Guy Kaner

The road to Timbuktu: travel poems (AuthorHouse, 2012)
Terra Treblinka: Poems of the Holocaust (AuthorHouse, 2012)
We pass each other on the stairs: 120 imaginary and real
    encounters (AuthorHouse, 2013)
Sirocco and scorpions: poems of Israel and Palestine (Aldrich
    Press, 2014)
A hawk in midflight: haiku and micro poems (AuthorHouse, 2017)
Back to Terezin: Holocaust poems (AuthorHouse, 2019)
Springtime in Moldova: poems of fantasy and dreams (Kelsay
    Books, 2019)
NoKaddish: poems in the Void (Ben Yehuda Press, 2020)
Twilight Passages: Death Poems (AuthorHouse, 2020)
A green cow (Hebrew)

About the Author

Hanoch Guy Kaner, Ph.D., Ed.D., spent his childhood and youth in Israel. He is a bilingual poet in Hebrew and English. He is an emeritus professor of Jewish and Hebrew literature at Temple University, and he has taught poetry and mentored at the Musehouse Center. His poetry has been published in the U.S., England, Wales, Greece and Israel. He has won awards in *Poetica, Mad Poets Society, Poetry Superhighway* and *Philadelphia Poets.* His book *Terra Treblinka* was a finalist in the Northbrook Poetry Contest.

Hanoch Guy Kaner is the author of nine English poetry collections and a Hebrew poetry collection.